Manners Matter

10 table manners every child should know.

A Note to Parents ...

Eating a meal together as a family can be a wonderful opportunity for building closer relationships and having fun at the same time! Our book, "Manners Matter" can help you begin conversation with your youngster about proper table manners and why they are important. We encourage you to have fun with these. Here are some suggestions:

* Let your children ask questions.
* Point out the numbers as well as the words and pictures.
* Maybe even act out one of the 10 table manners before dinner.
* Practice one of the Table Manners for one whole week.

We hope you have as much fun teaching table manners to your children as we did putting together this book!

ENJOY!

This Book Belongs To

_____

From high chair to table
my parents know best,

"You must learn your manners
to sit with the rest."

"Please come to the table
when you are first told,

Or else your whole dinner
will quickly get cold."

#1

"Make sure you say grace
and give thanks to our God,

Yes, even when eating a bean
or pea pod."

#2

3

"Sit like a soldier;
your napkin on lap,

Feet on the floor
and take off your cap."

#4

"When eating with FAMILY
don't buzz like a bee,

Talk with each other;
turn off the T.V."

"'Please pass the bread,'
remember to utter,

Don't sneak dessert
or stick forks in the butter!"

5

"You must close your mouth
when chewing your food,

'Cause talking while eating
can be very rude."

#6

7

"When sipping your soup
you should try not to slurp,

And tell the cook 'Thanks!'
but don't use a burp."

8

"While eating your food
don't be caught a'smackin,

Or off to your room
you'll be sent a'packin'."

"No ugly sounds
should you ever make,

Save it for bath bubbles;
for goodness sake!"

#9

"Clear all your dishes
right after the meal,

It's the least you can do
and it's not a big deal."

#10

"As you grow older
you'll learn to be able,

To have proper manners
when you're at the table."

THE END

49512580R00018

Made in the USA
Middletown, DE
18 October 2017